·Cooking for Today·

INDIAN VEGETARIAN COOKING

·*Cooking for Today*·

INDIAN VEGETARIAN COOKING

LOUISE STEELE

Distributed in the USA by SMITHMARK Publishers,
a division of U.S. Media Holdings Inc.,
16, East 32nd Street, New York, NY 10016

SMITHMARK books are available for bulk purchase for sales promotion and premium use.
For details, write or call the Manager of Special Sales, SMITHMARK publishers,
16 East 32nd Street, New York, NY 10016; (212) 532-6600

ISBN 0-7651-9851-7

10 9 8 7 6 5 4 3 2 1

Printed in Italy

Acknowledgements:

Design & DTP: Pedro & Frances Prá-Lopez / Kingfisher Design
Art Direction: Clive Hayball
Managing Editor: Alexa Stace
Special Photography: Martin Brigdale
Home Economist: Jill Eggleton
Step-by-Step Photography: Karl Adamson
Step-by-Step Home Economist: Joanna Craig
Stylist: Helen Trent

Photographs on pages 6, 28, 46, & 64: By courtesy of ZEFA

Note:
*Cup measurements in this book are for American cups. Tablespoons are assumed to be 15 ml. Unless otherwise
stated, milk is assumed to be full-fat, eggs are AA extra large, and pepper is freshly ground black pepper.*

Contents

⚜

CHAPTER ONE

Soups & Appetizers

If a dessert is the crowning grand finale to a meal then an appetizer must be the opening overture, and should be orchestrated to tease the tastebuds and tempt the appetite. The repertoire of vegetarian Indian dishes to fulfil this role is fortunately wide and varied. Soups are a natural choice for the prepare-ahead cook and can be made thick and hearty with legumes like beans and lentils to satisfy large appetites. Some soups, like Indian Bean Soup (see page 8) and Spicy Dal and Carrot Soup (see page 12) will also double up beautifully as light lunch dishes. Others provide a lighter, more refreshing start, as in Minted Pea and Yogurt Soup (see page 11).

In India, appetizers are rarely served as such, and would instead accompany a meal. These typical dishes do, however, fill the role of appetizers and are just perfect to serve with drinks at informal buffet parties. Vegetable and Cashew Samosas (see page 19) and Garlicky Mushroom Pakoras (see page 16) can be made well ahead and reheated before serving, and Spiced Corn & Nut Mix (see page 14) makes a superb alternative to the predictable peanut and crisp offerings with drinks.

Opposite: *Transporting supplies by canoe in Kerala.*

STEP 1

STEP 2

STEP 3

STEP 4

INDIAN BEAN SOUP

A thick and hearty soup, nourishing and substantial enough to serve as a main meal with whole-wheat bread. Black-eye peas are used here, but red kidney beans or chick-peas may be added to the mixture if preferred.

SERVES 4–6

4 tbsp ghee or vegetable oil
2 onions, peeled and chopped
1½ cups potato, peeled and cut into chunks
1½ cups parsnip, peeled and cut into chunks
1½ cups turnip or rutabaga, peeled and cut
    into chunks
2 celery stalks, trimmed and sliced
2 zucchini, trimmed and sliced
1 green bell pepper, deseeded and cut into
    ½-in. pieces
2 garlic cloves, crushed
2 tsp ground coriander
1 tbsp paprika
1 tbsp mild curry paste
5 cups vegetable stock
salt
14 ounce can black-eye peas, drained and
    rinsed
chopped fresh cilantro, to garnish (optional)

1 Heat the ghee or oil in a saucepan, add all the prepared vegetables, except the zucchini and green bell pepper, and cook over a moderate heat for 5 minutes, stirring frequently. Add the garlic, cilantro, paprika, and curry paste and cook for 1 minute, stirring.

2 Stir in the stock and season with salt to taste. Bring to a boil, cover, and simmer gently for 25 minutes, stirring occasionally.

3 Stir in the peas, sliced zucchini, and green bell pepper, cover, and continue cooking for a further 15 minutes or until all the vegetables are tender.

4 Purée 1¼ cups of the soup mixture (about 2 ladlefuls) in a food processor or blender. Return the puréed mixture to the soup in the pot and reheat until piping hot. Sprinkle with chopped cilantro, if using and serve hot.

COOK'S TIP

For a thinner, broth-type consistency to the soup, do not purée the 2 ladlefuls of mixture as instructed in step 4. The flavor of this soup improves if made the day before it is required, as this allows time for all the flavors to blend and develop.

MINTED PEA & YOGURT SOUP

A deliciously refreshing soup that is full of goodness. It is also extremely tasty served chilled – in which case, you may like to thin the consistency a little more with extra stock, yogurt, or milk.

STEP 1

SERVES 6

2 tbsp ghee or vegetable oil
2 onions, peeled and coarsely chopped
1½ cups potato, peeled and coarsely chopped
2 garlic cloves, peeled
1-in. piece gingerroot, chopped
1 tsp ground cilantro
1 tsp ground cumin
1 tbsp all-purpose flour
3½ cups vegetable stock
3 cups frozen peas
2–3 tbsp chopped fresh mint, to taste
⅔ cup plain yogurt
½ tsp cornstarch
1¼ cups milk
salt and freshly ground black pepper
a little extra yogurt, for serving (optional)
mint sprigs, to garnish

gently for 15 minutes or until the vegetables are tender.

3 Purée the soup, in batches, in a blender or food processor. Return the mixture to the pot and season well with salt and pepper to taste. Blend the yogurt with the cornstarch and stir into the soup.

4 Add the milk and bring almost to a boil, stirring all the time. Cook very gently for 2 minutes. Serve hot, sprinkled with the remaining mint and a swirl of extra yogurt, if wished.

STEP 2

STEP 3a

1 Heat the ghee or oil in a saucepan, add the onions and potato, and cook gently for 3 minutes. Stir in the garlic, ginger, cilantro, cumin, and flour and cook for 1 minute, stirring.

2 Add the stock, peas, and half the mint and bring to a boil, stirring. Reduce the heat, cover, and simmer

COOK'S TIP

The yogurt is mixed with a little cornstarch before being added to the hot soup – this helps to stabilize the yogurt and prevents it from separating when heated.

STEP 3b

STEP 1

STEP 2

STEP 3

STEP 4

SPICY DAL & CARROT SOUP

This delicious, warming, and nutritious soup uses split red lentils and carrots as the two main ingredients, and includes a selection of spices to give it a "kick." It is simple to make and extremely good to eat.

SERVES 6

$^2/_3$ cup split red lentils
5 cups vegetable stock
2 cups carrots, peeled and sliced
2 onions, peeled and chopped
1 cup canned chopped tomatoes
2 garlic cloves, peeled and chopped
2 tbsp vegetable ghee or oil
1 tsp ground cumin
1 tsp ground cilantro
1 fresh green chili, deseeded and chopped, or
    use 1 tsp minced chili (from a jar)
$^1/_2$ tsp ground turmeric
1 tbsp lemon juice
salt
$1^1/_4$ cups milk
2 tbsp chopped fresh cilantro
yogurt, to serve

1 Place the lentils in a strainer and wash well under cold running water. Drain and place in a large saucepan with 3½ cups of the stock, the carrots, onions, tomatoes, and garlic. Bring the mixture to a boil, reduce the heat, cover, and simmer for 30 minutes or until the vegetables and lentils are tender.

2 Meanwhile, heat the ghee or oil in a small saucepan. Add the cumin, cilantro, chili, and turmeric and fry gently for 1 minute. Remove from the heat and stir in the lemon juice and salt to taste.

3 Purée the soup in batches in a blender or food processor. Return the soup to the pot, add the spice mixture and the remaining stock or water, and simmer for 10 minutes.

4 Add the milk, and taste and adjust the seasoning, if necessary. Stir in the chopped cilantro and reheat gently. Serve hot, with a swirl of yogurt.

VARIATION

As this soup has quite a hot and spicy flavor, it may be wise to omit or at least reduce the amount of chili in the recipe when serving it to children. A spoonful of plain yogurt, swirled into each serving of soup makes it extra nutritious and delicious.

STEP 1a

STEP 2

STEP 3

STEP 4

SPICED CORN & NUT MIX

A flavorful mixture of buttery-spiced nuts, raisins, and popcorn to enjoy as a snack or with pre-dinner drinks.

SERVES 6

2 tbsp vegetable oil
¼ cup popping corn
¼ cup butter
1 garlic clove, crushed
⅓ cup unblanched almonds
½ cup unsalted cashews
½ cup unsalted peanuts
1 tsp Worcestershire sauce
1 tsp curry powder or paste
¼ tsp chili powder
⅓ cup seedless raisins
salt

1 Heat the oil in a saucepan. Add the popping corn, stir well, then cover, and cook over a fairly high heat for 3–5 minutes, holding the saucepan lid firmly and shaking the pan frequently until the popping stops.

2 Turn the popped corn into a dish, discarding any unpopped corn kernels.

3 Melt the butter in a skillet, add the garlic, almonds, cashews, and peanuts, then stir in the Worcestershire sauce, curry powder or paste, and chili powder, and cook over medium heat for 2–3 minutes, stirring frequently.

4 Remove the skillet from the heat and stir in the raisins and popped corn. Season with salt to taste and mix well. Transfer to a serving bowl and serve warm or cold.

VARIATIONS

Use a mixture of any unsalted nuts of your choice – walnuts, pecans, hazelnuts, Brazil nuts, macadamia nuts, and pine nuts are all delicious prepared this way. For a less fiery flavor omit the curry powder and chili powder and add 1 tsp cumin seeds, 1 tsp ground cilantro, and ½ tsp paprika. Sprinkle with 1–2 tbsp of chopped fresh cilantro just before serving.

STEP 1

STEP 2

STEP 3

STEP 4

GARLICKY MUSHROOM PAKORAS

Whole mushrooms are dunked in a spiced garlicky batter and deep-fried until golden. They are at their most delicious served hot and freshly cooked.

SERVES 6

1½ cups gram flour (see box)
½ tsp salt
¼ tsp baking powder
1 tsp cumin seeds
½–1 tsp chili powder, to taste
¾ cup water
2 garlic cloves, crushed
1 small onion, peeled and finely chopped
vegetable oil, for deep-frying
1 pound button mushrooms, trimmed and wiped
kosher salt, to serve
lemon wedges and cilantro sprigs, to garnish

1 Put the gram flour, salt, baking powder, cumin, and chili powder into a bowl and mix well together. Make a well in the center of the mixture and gradually stir in the water, mixing to form a batter.

2 Stir the crushed garlic and the chopped onion into the batter and leave the mixture to infuse for 10 minutes. One-third fill a deep-fat fryer or pan with vegetable oil and heat to 350°F or until hot enough to brown a cube of day-old bread in 30 seconds. Lower the basket into the hot oil.

3 Meanwhile, mix the mushrooms into the batter, stirring to coat. Remove a few at a time and place them into the hot oil. Fry for about 2 minutes or until golden brown.

4 Remove from the pot with a slotted spoon and drain on paper towels while cooking the remainder in the same way. Serve hot, sprinkled with kosher salt and garnished with lemon wedges and cilantro sprigs.

GRAM FLOUR

Gram flour (also known as besan flour) is a pale yellow flour made from chick peas. It is now readily available from larger supermarkets as well as Indian food stores and some ethnic delicatessens. Gram flour is also used to make onion bhajis.

VEGETABLE & CASHEW SAMOSAS

These delicious little fried pastries are really quite simple to make.
Serve them hot as an appetizer to an Indian meal or cold as
a well-flavored picnic or lunch-box snack.

STEP 1

MAKES 12

2 cups potatoes, peeled and diced
1 cup frozen peas
3 tbsp vegetable oil
1 onion, peeled and chopped
1-in. piece gingerroot, chopped
1 garlic clove, crushed
1 tsp garam masala
2 tsp mild curry paste
$1/2$ tsp cumin seeds
2 tsp lemon juice
$1/2$ cup unsalted cashews, coarsely chopped
vegetable oil, for shallow frying
salt
cilantro sprigs, to garnish
mango chutney, to serve

PASTRY:

2 cups all-purpose flour
$1/4$ cup butter, diced
6 tbsp warm milk

1 Cook the potatoes in a saucepan of boiling, salted water for 5 minutes. Add the peas and cook for a further 4 minutes or until the potato is tender. Drain well. Heat the oil in a skillet, add the onion, potato and pea mixture, ginger, garlic, and spices, and fry for 2 minutes. Stir in the lemon juice and

STEP 2

cook gently, uncovered, for 2 minutes. Remove from the heat, slightly mash the potato and peas, then add the cashews, mix well, and season with salt.

2 To make the dough, put the flour in a bowl and rub in the butter finely. Mix in the milk to form a dough. Knead lightly and divide into 6 portions. Form each into a ball and roll out on a lightly floured surface to an 7 in. circle. Cut each one in half.

3 Divide the filling equally between each semicircle of dough, spreading it out to within $1/4$ in. of the edges. Brush the edges of dough all the way around with water and fold over to form triangular shapes, sealing the edges well together to enclose the filling completely.

STEP 3

4 One-third fill a large, deep skillet with oil and heat to 350°F or until hot enough to brown a cube of bread in 30 seconds. Fry the samosas, a few at a time, turning frequently until golden brown and heated through. Drain on paper towels and keep warm while cooking the remainder in the same way. Garnish with a few cilantro sprigs and serve hot.

STEP 4

CHAPTER TWO

Main Dishes

India has long stood as the undisputed centre of vegetarianism. This is partly due to religious reasons (Hindus are forbidden meat), and partly due to economic factors. The vegetarian dishes they eat therefore supply all the proteins, vitamins, and minerals that the human body needs.

The Indians make great use and show creative flair in using their staples of rice, lentils, fruit, nuts, eggs, milk, legumes, and vegetables to make a seemingly endless array of dishes from biryanis and curries to pilaus and paneers that delight the appetite.

Such basic foodstuffs are used to create spicy, wholesome curries; stuffed vegetable treats using eggplants and potatoes; rice and vegetable pilaus with crunchy nut crowns; and nut and lentil "meatballs" better known as koftas. Mixed and matched with flavorsome rice, lentil, vegetable, and bread accompaniments, they make a nutritious feast for the vegetarian.

Opposite: *Plowing a rice paddy with the help of water buffaloes, near Madras.*

STEP 1

STEP 2

STEP 3

STEP 4

EGG & LENTIL CURRY

*A nutritious meal that is easy and relatively quick to make. The curried
lentil sauce is also delicious served with cooked vegetables
such as cauliflower, potatoes, or eggplants.*

SERVES 4

3 tbsp ghee or vegetable oil
1 large onion, peeled and chopped
2 garlic cloves, chopped
1-in. piece gingerroot, chopped
$\frac{1}{2}$ tsp minced chili (from a jar), or use
    chili powder
1 tsp ground cilantro
1 tsp ground cumin
1 tsp paprika
$\frac{1}{2}$ cup split red lentils
$1\frac{3}{4}$ cups vegetable stock
1 cup canned chopped tomatoes
6 eggs
$\frac{1}{4}$ cup coconut milk
salt
2 tomatoes, cut into wedges, and cilantro
    sprigs, to garnish
parathas, chapatis, or naan bread, to serve

1 Heat the ghee or oil in a saucepan,
add the onion, and fry gently for
3 minutes. Stir in the garlic, ginger, chili,
and spices and cook gently for 1 minute,
stirring frequently. Stir in the lentils,
stock, and chopped tomatoes and bring
to a boil. Reduce the heat, cover, and
simmer gently for 30 minutes, stirring
occasionally until the lentils and onion
are tender.

2 Meanwhile, place the eggs in a
separate pot of cold water and
bring to a boil. Reduce the heat and
simmer for 10 minutes. Drain and cover
immediately with cold water.

3 Stir the coconut milk into the lentil
mixture and season well with salt
to taste. Purée the mixture in a blender
or food processor until smooth. Return to
the pot and heat through.

4 Shell and cut the hard-boiled eggs
in half lengthwise. Arrange 3
halves, in a petal design, on each serving
plate. Spoon the hot lentil sauce over the
eggs, adding enough to flood the serving
plate. Arrange a tomato wedge and a
cilantro sprig between each halved egg.
Serve hot with parathas, chapatis, or
naan bread to mop up the sauce.

COOK'S NOTE

Eggs contain high quality protein, fat, iron,
and Vitamins A, B, and D, although they
are also high in cholesterol. Incidentally, a
brown-shelled egg and a rich yellow yolk
has exactly the same nutritional value as a
white egg.

STEP 1

STEP 2

STEP 3

STEP 4

BROWN RICE WITH FRUIT & NUTS

Here is a delicious and filling rice dish that is nice and spicy and includes fruits for a refreshing flavor and toasted nuts for an interesting crunchy texture.

SERVES 4–6

4 tbsp ghee or vegetable oil
1 large onion, peeled and chopped
2 garlic cloves, crushed
1-in. piece gingerroot, chopped
1 tsp chili powder
1 tsp cumin seeds
1 tbsp mild or medium curry powder or paste
1½ cups long-grain brown rice
3¾ cups boiling vegetable stock
14 ounce can chopped tomatoes
1½ cups ready-soaked dried apricots or
    peaches, cut into slivers
1 red bell pepper, cored, deseeded, and diced
¾ cup frozen peas
1–2 small, slightly green bananas
⅓–½ cup toasted nuts (a mixture of almonds,
    cashews, and hazelnuts, or pine nuts)
salt and freshly ground black pepper
cilantro sprigs, to garnish

1 Heat the ghee or oil in a large saucepan, add the onion, and fry gently for 3 minutes. Stir in the garlic, ginger, spices, and rice and cook gently for 2 minutes, stirring all the time until the rice is coated in the spiced oil.

2 Pour in the boiling stock and add the canned tomatoes and season with salt and pepper to taste. Bring to a boil, then reduce the heat, cover, and simmer gently for 40 minutes or until the rice is almost cooked and most of the liquid is absorbed.

3 Add the slivered apricots or peaches, diced red bell pepper, and peas. Cover and continue cooking for 10 minutes. Remove from the heat and allow to stand for 5 minutes without uncovering.

4 Peel and slice the bananas. Uncover the rice mixture and fork through to mix the ingredients together. Add the toasted nuts and sliced banana and toss lightly. Transfer to a warm serving platter and garnish with cilantro sprigs. Serve hot.

COOK'S NOTE

Brown rice has a delicious nutty flavor and a more chewy texture than white rice. And because the germ of the grain is retained, it also contains larger amounts of vitamins, minerals, and protein. Brown rice takes longer to cook than white rice.

MUTTAR PANEER

Paneer is a delicious fresh, soft cheese frequently used in Indian cooking. It is easily made at home, but remember to make it the day before required.

SERVES 6

²/₃ cup vegetable oil
2 onions, peeled and chopped
2 garlic cloves, crushed
1-in. piece gingerroot, chopped
1 tsp garam masala
1 tsp ground turmeric
1 tsp chili powder
3 cups frozen peas
1 cup canned chopped tomatoes
¹/₂ cup vegetable stock
salt and freshly ground black pepper
2 tbsp chopped fresh cilantro

PANEER:

2¹/₂ quarts whole milk
5 tbsp lemon juice
1 garlic clove, crushed (optional)
1 tbsp chopped fresh cilantro (optional)

1 Bring the milk to a rolling boil in a large saucepan. Remove from the heat and stir in the lemon juice. Return to the heat for about 1 minute until the curds and whey separate. Remove from the heat. Line a colander with double thickness cheesecloth and pour the mixture through the cheesecloth, adding the garlic and cilantro, if using. Squeeze all the liquid from the curds and leave to drain.

2 Transfer to a dish, cover with a plate and weights, and leave overnight in the refrigerator.

3 Cut the pressed paneer into small cubes. Heat the oil in a large skillet, add the paneer cubes, and fry until golden on all sides. Remove from the pan and drain on paper towels.

4 Pour off some of the oil, leaving about 4 tablespoons in the skillet. Add the onions, garlic, and ginger and fry gently for about 5 minutes, stirring frequently. Stir in the spices and fry gently for 2 minutes. Add the peas, tomatoes, and stock and season with salt and pepper. Cover and simmer for 10 minutes, stirring occasionally, until the onion is tender. Add the fried paneer cubes and cook for a further 5 minutes. Taste and adjust the seasoning, if necessary. Sprinkle with the cilantro and serve at once.

STEP 2

STEP 3

STEP 4

STEP 5

SPLIT PEAS WITH VEGETABLES

Here is a simple, yet nourishing and flavorful way of cooking yellow split peas. Vary the selection of vegetables and spices according to personal preferences.

SERVES 4–5

1$^1/_3$ cup dried yellow split peas
5 cups cold water
$^1/_2$ tsp ground turmeric (optional)
1 pound new potatoes, scrubbed
5 tbsp vegetable oil
2 onions, peeled and coarsely chopped
2$^1/_2$ cups button mushrooms, wiped
1 tsp ground cilantro
1 tsp ground cumin
1 tsp chili powder
1 tsp garam masala
1$^3/_4$ cups vegetable stock
$^1/_2$ cauliflower, broken into flowerets
$^2/_3$ cup frozen peas
6 ounces cherry tomatoes
salt and freshly ground black pepper
halved mint sprigs, to garnish

1 Place the split peas in a bowl, add the cold water, and leave to soak for at least 4 hours or overnight.

2 Place the peas and the soaking liquid in a fairly large saucepan, stir in the turmeric, if using, and bring to a boil. Skim off any surface scum, half-cover the pan with a lid, and simmer gently for 20 minutes or until the peas are tender and almost dry. Remove the pot from the heat and reserve.

3 Meanwhile, cut the potatoes into $^1/_4$ in. slices. Heat the oil in a flameproof casserole, add the onions, potatoes, and mushrooms, and cook gently for 5 minutes, stirring frequently. Stir in the spices and fry gently for 1 minute, then add salt and pepper to taste, the stock, and cauliflower flowerets.

4 Cover and simmer gently for 25 minutes or until the potato is tender, stirring occasionally. Add the split peas (and any of the cooking liquid) and the frozen peas. Bring to a boil, cover, and continue cooking for 5 minutes.

5 Stir in the halved cherry tomatoes and cook for 2 minutes. Taste and adjust the seasoning, if necessary. Serve hot, garnished with mint sprigs.

VARIATION

Chana dal (popular with vegetarians because of its high-protein content) may be used instead of yellow split peas, if preferred. *Chana dal* is similar to yellow split peas, although the grains are smaller and the flavor sweeter.

28

STUFFED EGGPLANTS

These are delicious served hot or cold, topped with plain yogurt or cucumber and yogurt combined.

STEP 1

SERVES 6

OVEN: 350°F

1⅓ cups continental lentils
3¾ cups water
2 garlic cloves, crushed
3 well-shaped eggplants, leaf ends trimmed
⅔ cup vegetable oil
2 onions, peeled and chopped
4 tomatoes, chopped
2 tsp cumin seeds
1 tsp ground cinnamon
2 tbsp mild curry paste
1 tsp minced chili (from a jar)
2 tbsp chopped fresh mint
salt and freshly ground black pepper
plain yogurt and mint sprigs, to serve

1 Rinse the lentils under cold running water. Drain and place in a saucepan with the water and garlic. Cover and simmer for 30 minutes.

2 Cook the eggplants in a separate pot of boiling water for 5 minutes. Drain, then plunge into cold water for 5 minutes. Drain again, then cut the eggplants in half lengthwise, and scoop out most of the flesh and reserve, leaving a ½ in. thick border to form a shell.

3 Place the eggplant shells in a shallow greased ovenproof dish, brush with a little oil, and sprinkle with salt and pepper. Cook in the preheated oven for 10 minutes. Meanwhile, heat half the remaining oil in a skillet, add the onions and tomatoes, and fry gently for 5 minutes. Chop the reserved eggplant flesh, add to the skillet with the spices, and cook gently for 5 minutes. Season with salt.

4 Stir in the lentils, most of the remaining oil, reserving a little, and the mint. Spoon the mixture into the shells. Drizzle with the remaining oil and bake for 15 minutes. Serve hot or cold topped with a spoonful of plain yogurt and mint sprigs.

STEP 2

STEP 3

COOK'S TIP

Choose nice plump eggplants rather than thin tapering ones because they retain their shape better when baked with a stuffing.

STEP 4

31

STEP 1a

STEP 1b

STEP 2

STEP 3

LENTIL & VEGETABLE BIRYANI

The delicious mix of vegetables, basmati rice, and lentils produces this wholesome and nutritious dish.

SERVES 6

²/₃ cup lentils
4 tbsp ghee or vegetable oil
2 onions, peeled, quartered, and sliced
2 garlic cloves, crushed
1-in. piece gingerroot, chopped
1 tsp ground turmeric
¹/₂ tsp chili powder
1 tsp ground cilantro
2 tsp ground cumin
3 tomatoes, skinned and chopped
1 eggplant trimmed, and cut in ¹/₂-in. pieces
6¹/₄ cups boiling vegetable stock
1 red or green bell pepper, cored, deseeded, and diced
1³/₄ cups basmati rice
1 cup thin green beans, topped, tailed, and halved
1¹/₃ cups cauliflower flowerets
1¹/₂ cups mushrooms, wiped and sliced or quartered
¹/₂ cup unsalted cashews
3 hard-boiled eggs, shelled, to garnish
cilantro sprigs, to garnish

1 Rinse the lentils under cold running water and drain. Heat the ghee or oil in a saucepan, add the onions, and fry gently for 2 minutes. Stir in the garlic, ginger, and spices and fry gently for 1 minute, stirring frequently. Add the lentils, tomatoes, eggplant, and 2½ cups of the stock, mix well, then cover, and simmer gently for 20 minutes. Add the red or green bell pepper and cook for a further 10 minutes or until the lentils are tender and all the liquid has been absorbed.

2 Meanwhile, place the rice in a strainer and rinse under cold running water until the water runs clear. Drain and place in another pot with the remaining stock. Bring to a boil, add the green beans, cauliflower, and mushrooms, then cover, and cook gently for 15 minutes or until the rice and the vegetables are tender. Remove from the heat and leave, covered, for 10 minutes.

3 Add the lentil mixture and the cashews to the cooked rice and mix lightly together. Pile onto a warm serving platter and garnish with wedges of hard-boiled egg and cilantro sprigs. Serve hot.

STEP 1

STEP 2

STEP 3a

STEP 3b

BAKED POTATOES WITH BEANS

Baked potatoes, topped with a mixture of beans in a
spicy sauce, provide a deliciously filling, high-fiber dish.

SERVES 6
OVEN: 400°F

6 large baking potatoes
4 tbsp vegetable ghee or oil
1 large onion, peeled and chopped
2 garlic cloves, crushed
1 tsp ground turmeric
1 tbsp cumin seeds
2 tbsp mild or medium curry paste
12 ounces cherry tomatoes
14 ounce can black-eye peas, drained and
    rinsed
14 ounce can red kidney beans, drained and
    rinsed
1 tbsp lemon juice
2 tbsp tomato paste
2/3 cup water
2 tbsp chopped fresh mint or cilantro
salt and freshly ground black pepper
plain yogurt, to serve
mint or cilantro sprigs, to garnish

1 Wash and scrub the potatoes and
    prick several times with a fork.
Place in the oven and bake for 1–1¼
hours or until the potatoes feel soft when
gently squeezed.

2 About 20 minutes before the end of
    cooking time, prepare the topping.
Heat the ghee or oil in a saucepan, add

the onion, and cook gently for 5 minutes,
stirring frequently. Add the garlic,
turmeric, cumin seeds, and curry paste
and cook gently for 1 minute. Stir in the
tomatoes, black-eye peas, red kidney
beans, lemon juice, tomato paste, water,
and chopped mint or cilantro. Season
with salt and pepper, then cover, and
cook gently for 10 minutes, stirring
frequently.

3 When the potatoes are cooked, cut
    them in half and mash the flesh
lightly with a fork. Spoon the prepared
bean mixture on top, garnish with mint
or cilantro sprigs, and serve with a dish of
plain yogurt.

VARIATION

Instead of cutting the potatoes in half, cut
a cross in each and squeeze gently to
open out. Spoon some of the prepared
filling into the cross and place any
remaining filling on the side.

STEP 1

STEP 2

STEP 3

STEP 4

SPINACH & EGGPLANT

*This interesting combination of lentils and spiced vegetables is
delicious served with parathas, chapatis, or naan bread,
plus a bowl of plain yogurt.*

SERVES 4

1¹/₃ cup split red lentils
3 cups water
1 onion
1 eggplant
1 red bell pepper
2 zucchini
4 ounces mushrooms, wiped
¹/₂ pound leaf spinach
4 tbsp vegetable ghee or oil
1 fresh green chili, deseeded and chopped, or
    use 1 tsp minced chili (from a jar)
1 tsp ground cumin
1 tsp ground cilantro
1-in. piece gingerroot, chopped
²/₃ cup vegetable stock
salt
cilantro or flat-leaved parsley sprigs, to
    garnish

1 Wash the lentils and place in a
saucepan with the water. Cover
and simmer for 15 minutes until the
lentils are soft but still whole.

2 Meanwhile, peel, quarter, and slice
the onion. Trim the leaf end off the
eggplant and cut into ½-in. pieces.
Remove the stem end and seeds from the
bell pepper and cut into ½-in. pieces. Trim
and cut the zucchini into ½-in. thick

slices. Thickly slice the mushrooms.
Discard the coarse stems from the
spinach leaves and wash the spinach.

3 Heat the ghee or oil in a large
saucepan, add the onion and red
bell pepper, and fry gently for 3 minutes,
stirring frequently. Stir in the eggplant,
zucchini, mushrooms, chili, spices, and
ginger and fry gently for 1 minute. Add
the spinach and stock and season with
salt to taste. Stir until the spinach leaves
wilt down. Cover and simmer for
10 minutes or until the vegetables
are just tender.

4 Make a border of the lentils on a
warm serving plate and spoon the
vegetable mixture into the center. (The
lentils may be stirred into the vegetable
mixture, instead of being used as a
border, if wished.) Garnish with cilantro
or flat-leaved parsley sprigs.

SPINACH

Wash the spinach thoroughly in several
changes of cold water because it can be
gritty. Drain well and shake off excess
water from the leaves before adding to
the pot.

STEP 2

STEP 3

STEP 4

STEP 5

VEGETABLE, NUT, & LENTIL KOFTAS

This mixture is shaped into golf-ball shapes and baked in the oven with a sprinkling of aromatic garam masala. These are delicious served hot or cold with a yogurt dressing and chapatis.

SERVES 4–5
OVEN: 350°F

6 tbsp vegetable ghee or oil
1 onion, peeled and finely chopped
2 carrots, peeled and finely chopped
2 celery stalks, trimmed and finely chopped
2 garlic cloves, crushed
1 fresh green chili, deseeded and finely
   chopped
1 1/2 tbsp curry powder or paste
1 1/3 cups split red lentils
2 1/2 cups vegetable stock
2 tbsp tomato paste
2 cups fresh whole wheat bread crumbs
3/4 cup unsalted cashews, finely chopped
2 tbsp chopped fresh cilantro or parsley
1 egg, beaten
salt and freshly ground black pepper
garam masala, for sprinkling

YOGURT DRESSING:
1 cup plain yogurt
1–2 tbsp chopped fresh cilantro or parsley
1–2 tbsp mango chutney, chopped if
   necessary

1 Heat 4 tablespoons of ghee or oil in a large saucepan and gently fry the onion, carrots, celery, garlic, and chili for 5 minutes, stirring frequently. Add the

curry powder or paste and the lentils and cook gently for 1 minute, stirring.

2 Add the stock and tomato paste and bring to a boil. Reduce the heat, cover, and simmer for 20 minutes or until the lentils are tender and all the liquid is absorbed.

3 Remove from the heat and cool slightly. Add the bread crumbs, nuts, cilantro, egg, and seasoning to taste. Mix well and leave to cool. Shape into balls about the size of golf balls. (The mixture is quite soft, so use 2 spoons to help shape the balls, if necessary.)

4 Place the balls on a greased cookie sheet, drizzle with the remaining oil, and sprinkle with a little garam masala, to taste. Cook in the preheated oven for 15–20 minutes or until piping hot and lightly golden.

5 Meanwhile, make the yogurt dressing. Mix all the ingredients together in a bowl. Serve the koftas hot with the yogurt dressing.

CHICK-PEAS & EGGPLANT

Canned chick-peas (widely available from supermarkets) are used in this dish, but you can use black-eye peas or red kidney beans if you prefer. Omit the chilies for a less fiery flavour.

STEP 1a

SERVES 4

1 large eggplant
2 zucchini
6 tbsp ghee or vegetable oil
1 large onion, peeled, quartered, and sliced
2 garlic cloves, crushed
1–2 fresh green chilies, deseeded and chopped, or use 1–2 tsp minced chili (from a jar)
2 tsp ground cilantro
2 tsp cumin seeds
1 tsp ground turmeric
1 tsp garam masala
14 ounce can chopped tomatoes
1¼ cups vegetable stock or water
14 ounce can chick-peas, drained and rinsed
2 tbsp chopped fresh mint
⅔ cup heavy cream
salt and freshly ground black pepper

STEP 1b

1 Trim the leaf end off the eggplant and cut into cubes. Trim and slice the zucchini. Heat the ghee or oil in a saucepan and gently fry the eggplant, zucchini, onion, garlic, and chilies for about 5 minutes, stirring and adding a little more oil to the pan, if necessary.

2 Stir in the spices and cook for 30 seconds. Add the tomatoes, stock, and salt and pepper to taste and cook for 10 minutes.

3 Add the chick-peas to the pot and continue cooking for a further 5 minutes. Stir in the mint and cream and reheat gently. Taste and adjust the seasoning, if necessary. Serve hot with plain or pilau rice, or with parathas, if preferred.

STEP 2

YOGURT

You could use plain yogurt instead of cream in this dish, in which case first blend it with ½ tsp cornstarch before adding to the pot and heating gently, stirring constantly. The cornstarch helps stabilize the yogurt to prevent it from separating during heating.

STEP 3

STEP 1

STEP 2

STEP 3

STEP 4

VEGETABLE CURRY

This colorful and interesting mixture of vegetables, cooked in a spicy sauce, is excellent served with pilau rice and naan bread. Vary the vegetables according to personal preferences.

SERVES 4

$^1/_2$ pound turnips or rutabaga, peeled
1 eggplant, leaf end trimmed
12 ounces new potatoes, scrubbed
$^1/_2$ pound cauliflower
$3^1/_2$ cups button mushrooms, wiped
1 large onion, peeled
$^1/_2$ pound carrots, peeled
6 tbsp ghee or vegetable oil
2 garlic cloves, crushed
2-in. piece gingerroot, chopped
1–2 fresh green chilies, deseeded and
*   chopped*
1 tbsp paprika
2 tsp ground cilantro
1 tbsp mild or medium curry powder or paste
$1^3/_4$ cups vegetable stock
14 ounce can chopped tomatoes
1 green bell pepper, deseeded and sliced
1 tbsp cornstarch
$^2/_3$ cup coconut milk
2–3 tbsp blanched almonds, finely ground
salt
cilantro sprigs, to garnish

1 Cut the turnips or rutabaga, eggplant, and potatoes into ½ in. cubes. Divide the cauliflower into small flowerets. Leave the mushrooms whole, or slice thickly, if preferred. Slice the onion and carrots.

2 Heat the ghee or oil in a large saucepan, add the onion, turnip, potato, and cauliflower, and cook gently for 3 minutes, stirring frequently. Add the garlic, ginger, chili, spices, and curry powder or paste and cook for 1 minute, stirring.

3 Add the stock, tomatoes, eggplant, and mushrooms and season with salt. Cover and simmer gently for about 30 minutes, or until tender, stirring occasionally. Add the green bell pepper, cover, and continue cooking for a further 5 minutes.

4 Smoothly blend the cornstarch with the coconut milk and stir into the mixture. Add the ground almonds and simmer for 2 minutes, stirring all the time. Taste and adjust the seasoning, if necessary. Serve hot, garnished with cilantro sprigs.

GROUND ALMONDS

The ground almonds used in this dish not only help to thicken the sauce but also add richness and flavor to it. For a less fiery flavor in the dish, reduce or omit the amount of chili used.

STEP 1

STEP 2

STEP 3

STEP 4

SPICED BASMATI PILAU

Omit the broccoli and mushrooms from this recipe if you require only a simple spiced pilau. The whole spices are not meant to be eaten and may be removed before serving, if wished.

SERVES 6

2¹/₂ cups basmati rice
6 ounces broccoli, trimmed
6 tbsp vegetable oil
2 large onions, peeled and chopped
3¹/₂ cups mushrooms, wiped and sliced
2 garlic cloves, crushed
6 cardamom pods, split
6 whole cloves
8 black peppercorns
1 cinnamon stick or piece of cassia bark
1 tsp ground turmeric
5 cups boiling vegetable stock or water
¹/₃ cup seedless raisins
¹/₂ cup unsalted pistachios, coarsely chopped
salt and freshly ground black pepper

1 Place the rice in a strainer and wash well under cold running water until the water runs clear. Drain. Trim off most of the broccoli stem and cut into small flowerets, then quarter the stem lengthwise, and cut diagonally into ½-in. pieces.

2 Heat the oil in a large saucepan, add the onions and broccoli stems, and cook gently for 3 minutes, stirring frequently. Add the mushrooms, rice, garlic, and spices and cook gently for 1 minute, stirring frequently until the rice is coated in spiced oil.

3 Add the boiling stock and season with salt and pepper. Stir in the broccoli flowerets and return the mixture to a boil. Cover, reduce the heat, and cook gently for 15 minutes without uncovering.

4 Remove from the heat and leave to stand for 5 minutes without uncovering. Add the raisins and pistachios and gently fork through to fluff up the grains. Serve hot.

VARIATION

For added richness, you could stir a spoonful of vegetable ghee through the rice mixture just before serving. A little diced red bell pepper and a few cooked peas or corn kernels forked through at step 4 add a colorful touch.

CHAPTER THREE

Accompaniments

Bread accompanies nearly every meal in the form of parathas, which are basically fried chapattis; Naan, or leavened baked bread; crisp and crunchy poppadoms, flavoured or plain; and puris, small rounds of deep-fried bread that are sometimes stuffed with savory ingredients.

Vegetable accompaniments come in all guises, as mixed curried dishes; as fritters, delicious with a spoonful of relish; and as bhajis, which are basically fried and spiced vegetables. They all contribute to give an Indian meal flavor and texture as well as extra nourishment.

Needless to say rice is a staple food and is served as a matter of course with virtually every meal. Experiment by cooking it in a little coconut milk with just a pinch of spices or garam masala to liven up plain boiled or steamed rice. Also consider serving spiced potatoes and cooked lentils as an alternative to rice – they make a welcome change and provide good nutrition.

Opposite: *A spice market in India.*

STEP 1

STEP 2a

STEP 2b

STEP 3

CURRIED OKRA

Okra, also known as bhindi and lady's fingers, are a favorite Indian vegetable. You can buy them in many supermarkets, as well as Asian food stores and specialist vegetable stores.

SERVES 4

1 pound fresh okra
4 tbsp ghee or vegetable oil
1 bunch scallions, trimmed and sliced
2 garlic cloves, crushed
2-in. piece gingerroot, chopped
1 tsp minced chili (from a jar)
1½ tsp ground cumin
1 tsp ground cilantro
1 tsp ground turmeric
1 cup canned chopped tomatoes
⅔ cup vegetable stock
1 tsp garam masala
salt and freshly ground black pepper
chopped fresh cilantro, to garnish

1 Wash the okra, trim off the stems, and pat dry. Heat the ghee or oil in a large saucepan, add the scallions, garlic, ginger, and chili and fry gently for 1 minute, stirring frequently.

2 Stir in the spices and fry gently for 30 seconds, then add the tomatoes, stock, and okra. Season with salt and pepper to taste and simmer for about 15 minutes, stirring and turning the mixture occasionally. The okra should be cooked but still a little crisp.

3 Sprinkle with the garam masala, taste and adjust the seasoning, if necessary. Garnish with the chopped cilantro and serve hot.

COOK'S TIP

If preferred, slice the okra into rings, add to the mixture (step 2), cover, and cook until tender-crisp, stirring occasionally. When you buy fresh okra, make sure the pods are not shriveled or do not have any brown spots. Once you get it home, it will keep for 3 days tightly wrapped in the refrigerator.

EGGPLANT IN SAFFRON SAUCE

*Here is a quick and simple, delicately spiced, and delicious
way to cook eggplant.*

STEP 1a

STEP 1b

STEP 2

STEP 3

SERVES 4

a good pinch of saffron strands, finely
   crushed
1 tbsp boiling water
1 large eggplant
3 tbsp vegetable oil
1 large onion, peeled and coarsely chopped
2 garlic cloves, crushed
1-in. piece gingerroot, chopped
1½ tbsp mild or medium curry paste
1 tsp cumin seeds
⅓ cup heavy cream
⅓ cup plain yogurt
2 tbsp mango chutney, chopped if necessary
salt and freshly ground black pepper

1 Place the saffron in a small bowl,
add the boiling water, and leave to
infuse for 5 minutes. Trim the leaf end off
the eggplant, cut lengthwise into
quarters, then into ½-in. thick slices.

2 Heat the oil in a large skillet, add
the onion, and cook gently for
3 minutes. Stir in the eggplant, garlic,
ginger, curry paste, and cumin and cook
gently for 3 minutes.

3 Stir in the saffron water, cream,
yogurt, and chutney and cook

gently for 8–10 minutes, stirring
frequently, until the eggplant is cooked
through and tender. Season with salt and
pepper to taste and serve hot.

YOGURT

You will find that yogurt adds a creamy
texture and pleasant tartness to this sauce.
If you are worried about it separating
when heated, add a tablespoonful at a
time and stir it in well before adding
another. A little cornstarch blended with
the yogurt before cooking, also helps
prevent it from separating when heated.

STEP 1a

STEP 1b

STEP 2

STEP 3

SPINACH & CAULIFLOWER BHAJI

*This excellent vegetable dish goes well with most Indian food –
and it is simple and quick cooking, too.*

SERVES 4

1 cauliflower
1 pound fresh spinach, washed, or 8 ounces
   frozen spinach, defrosted
4 tbsp ghee or vegetable oil
2 large onions, peeled and coarsely chopped
2 garlic cloves, crushed
1-in. piece gingerroot, chopped
1¼ tsp cayenne pepper, or to taste
1 tsp ground cumin
1 tsp ground turmeric
2 tsp ground cilantro
14 ounce can chopped tomatoes
1¼ cups vegetable stock
salt and freshly ground black pepper

1 Divide the cauliflower into small
flowerets, discarding the hard
central core. Trim the stems from
spinach leaves. Heat the ghee or oil in a
large saucepan, add the onions and
cauliflower flowerets, and fry the
vegetables gently for about 3 minutes,
stirring frequently.

2 Add the garlic, ginger, and spices
and cook gently for 1 minute. Stir
in the tomatoes and the stock and season
with salt and pepper. Bring to a boil,
cover, reduce the heat, and simmer
gently for 8 minutes.

3 Add the spinach to the pan, stirring
and turning to wilt the leaves.
Cover and simmer gently for about
8–10 minutes, stirring frequently until
the spinach has wilted and the
cauliflower is tender. Serve hot.

SPINACH

You may prefer to use frozen spinach in
this recipe, in which case you require
½ pound frozen leaf spinach which must be
defrosted and well drained before adding
to the mixture and heating through.

FRIED SPICED POTATOES

Deliciously good and a super accompaniment to almost any main course dish, although rather high in calories!

STEP 1

SERVES 4–6

2 onions, peeled and quartered
2-in. piece gingerroot, finely chopped
2 garlic cloves, peeled
2–3 tbsp mild or medium curry paste
4 tbsp water
1¹/₂ pounds new potatoes
vegetable oil, for deep frying
3 tbsp vegetable ghee or oil
¹/₃ cup plain yogurt
¹/₃ cup heavy cream
3 tbsp chopped fresh mint
salt and freshly ground black pepper
¹/₂ bunch scallions, trimmed and chopped, to garnish

1 Place the onions, ginger, garlic, curry paste, and water in a blender or food processor and process until smooth, scraping down the sides of machine and blending again, if necessary.

2 Cut the potatoes into quarters – the pieces need to be about 1 in. in size – and pat dry with paper towels. Heat the oil in a deep-fat fryer to 350°F and fry the potatoes, in batches, for about 5 minutes or until golden brown, turning. Remove from the pan and drain on paper towels.

3 Heat the ghee or oil in a large skillet, add the curry and onion mixture, and fry gently for 2 minutes, stirring all the time. Add the yogurt, cream, and 2 tablespoons of mint and mix well.

4 Add the fried potatoes and stir until coated in the sauce. Cook for a further 5–7 minutes or until heated through and the sauce has thickened, stirring frequently. Season with salt and pepper to taste and sprinkle with the remaining mint and sliced scallions. Serve immediately.

STEP 2

STEP 3

STEP 4

STEP 1

STEP 2

STEP 3

STEP 5

MIXED BELL PEPPER POORIS

Whole wheat pooris are easy to make and so good to eat served with a topping of spicy mixed bell peppers and yogurt. You may, of course, simply make the pooris to serve plain with other dishes, if wished.

SERVES 6

POORIS:
1 cup whole wheat flour
1 tbsp ghee or vegetable oil
2 good pinches of salt
1/3 cup hot water
vegetable oil, for shallow frying
plain yogurt, to serve
cilantro sprigs, to garnish

TOPPING:
4 tbsp vegetable ghee or oil
1 large onion, peeled, quartered, and thinly
    sliced
1/2 red bell pepper, deseeded and thinly sliced
1/2 green bell pepper, deseeded and thinly sliced
1/4 eggplant, cut lengthwise into 6 wedges
    and thinly sliced
1 garlic clove, crushed
1-in. piece gingerroot, chopped
1/2–1 tsp minced chili (from a jar)
2 tsp mild or medium curry paste
1 cup canned chopped tomatoes
salt

1 To make the pooris, put the flour in a bowl with the ghee or oil and salt. Add hot water and mix to form a soft dough. Knead gently, cover with a damp cloth, and leave for 30 minutes.

2 Meanwhile, prepare the topping. Heat the ghee or oil in a large saucepan, add the onion, bell peppers, eggplant, garlic, ginger, chili, and curry paste and fry gently for 5 minutes. Stir in the tomatoes and salt to taste and simmer gently, uncovered, for 5 minutes, stirring occasionally until the sauce thickens. Remove from the heat.

3 Knead the dough on a floured surface and divide into 6. Roll each piece into a circle. Each circle should have a diameter of about 6 inches. Cover each one as you finish rolling, to prevent it from drying out.

4 Heat about ½ in. oil in a large skillet. Add a poori, one at a time, and fry for about 15 seconds on each side until puffed and golden, turning frequently. Drain thoroughly on paper towels and keep warm while cooking the remainder in the same way.

5 Reheat the vegetable mixture. Place a poori on each serving plate and top with the vegetable mixture. Add a spoonful of yogurt to each one and garnish with cilantro sprigs. Serve hot.

STEP 1

STEP 2

STEP 3

STEP 4

SWEET HOT CARROTS & BEANS

Take care not to overcook the vegetables in this tasty dish – they are definitely at their best served tender-crisp. Remember to discard the whole dried chilies before serving the dish.

SERVES 4

1 pound young carrots, trimmed and peeled
    if necessary
1/2 pound thin green beans
1 bunch scallions, trimmed
4 tbsp vegetable ghee or oil
1 tsp ground cumin
1 tsp ground cilantro
3 cardamom pods, split and seeds removed
2 whole dried red chilies
2 garlic cloves, crushed
1–2 tsp honey, to taste
1 tsp lime or lemon juice
1/2 cup unsalted, toasted cashews
1 tbsp chopped fresh cilantro or parsley
salt and freshly ground black pepper
slices of lime or lemon and cilantro sprigs, to
    garnish

1 Cut the carrots lengthwise into quarters and then in half crosswise if very long. Top and tail the beans. Cut the spring onions into 2-in. pieces. Cook the carrots and beans in a saucepan containing a little boiling, salted water for 5–6 minutes according to how tender-crisp you like vegetables. Drain well.

2 Heat the ghee or oil in a large skillet, add the scallions, carrots, beans, cumin, cilantro, cardamom seeds, and whole dried chilies. Cook gently for 2 minutes, stirring frequently.

3 Stir in the garlic, honey, and lemon or lime juice and continue cooking for a further 2 minutes, stirring occasionally. Season to taste with salt and pepper. Remove and discard the whole chilies.

4 Sprinkle the vegetables with the toasted cashews and chopped cilantro, mix together lightly. Serve immediately, garnished with slices of lime or lemon and cilantro sprigs.

CARROTS

If the carrots are very slender, it may not be necessary to cut them into quarters. Simply trim the leafy ends, scrub well, and cook in the boiling, salted water for a minute or two before adding the green beans to ensure that all the vegetables cook evenly.

POTATO FRITTERS WITH RELISH

These are incredibly simple to make and sure to be popular served as a tempting snack or as an accompaniment to almost any Indian main course dish.

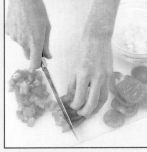

STEP 1

MAKES 8

½ cup whole wheat flour
½ tsp ground cilantro
½ tsp cumin seeds
¼ tsp chili powder
½ tsp ground turmeric
¼ tsp salt
1 egg
3 tbsp milk
12 ounces potatoes, peeled
1–2 garlic cloves, crushed
4 scallions, trimmed and chopped
½ cup whole-kernel corn
vegetable oil for shallow frying

ONION AND TOMATO RELISH:
1 onion, peeled
½ pound tomatoes
2 tbsp chopped fresh cilantro
2 tbsp chopped fresh mint
2 tbsp lemon juice
½ tsp roasted cumin seeds
¼ tsp salt
a few pinches of cayenne pepper, to taste

1 First make the relish. Cut the onion and tomatoes into small dice and place in a bowl with the remaining ingredients. Mix together well and leave to stand for at least 15 minutes before

serving to allow time for the flavors to blend.

2 Place the flour in a bowl, stir in the spices and salt, and make a well in the center. Add the egg and milk and mix to form a fairly thick batter.

STEP 2

3 Coarsely grate the potatoes, place in a strainer, and rinse well under cold running water. Drain and squeeze dry, then stir into the batter with the garlic, scallions, and corn.

4 Heat about ¼ in. oil in a large skillet and add a few tablespoonfuls of the mixture at a time, flattening each one to form a thin cake. Fry gently for 2–3 minutes or until golden brown and cooked through, turning frequently.

STEP 3

5 Drain on paper towels and keep hot while frying the remaining mixture in the same way. Serve hot with onion and tomato relish.

STEP 5